D0810329

Mindful thoughts for
BIRDWATCHERS

First published in the UK in 2018 by

Leaping Hare Press

An imprint of The Quarto Group
The Old Brewery, 6 Blundell Street
London N7 9BH, United Kingdom
T (0)20 7700 6700 **F** (0)20 7700 8066
www.QuartoKnows.com

British Library Cataloguing-in-Publication Data
A catalogue record for this book is available from the British Library

ISBN: 978-1-78240-645-7

This book was conceived, designed and produced by

Leaping Hare Press

58 West Street, Brighton BN1 2RA, UK

Publisher: *Susan Kelly*
Creative Director: *Michael Whitehead*
Editorial Director: *Tom Kitch*
Art Director: *James Lawrence*
Commissioning Editor: *Monica Perdoni*
Editor: *Claire Saunders*
Illustrator: *Lehel Kovac*
Editorial Assistant: *Niamh Jones*

Printed in Slovenia by GPS Group

1 3 5 7 9 10 8 6 4 2

Mindful thoughts for
BIRDWATCHERS

Finding awareness in nature

Adam Ford

Leaping Hare Press

Contents

We Share the World

With birds we have a window into the natural world. Birdwatching, with or without binoculars, can be one of the most accessible and enjoyable ways to meditate on the rich global ecosystem we inhabit. In this vast and ancient universe, the evolution of life on Earth, with all its biodiversity, is a miracle – and we, astonishingly, are part of it. We just need to give the mind a rest, to watch and listen.

There are almost 10,000 avian species, from the tiny bee hummingbird and pygmy kingfisher to the giant condor and wide-winged albatross. They float through our skies, dive deep in our oceans, lurk in the shadowy undergrowth of forests and stalk the open plains. They are everywhere. Getting to recognize and know them can be a source of pure delight. It can also give us a way to deepen our sense of conscious living, to become more aware of who we are and how we came to be here, and to be more mindful of our role as human beings sharing in the intricate web of life of this glorious but fragile world.

In birdwatching, we learn patience and how to be still – gentle skills much needed in the noisy, busy and anxiety-ridden modern life that many people are forced to endure. This book will explore the experience of birdwatching from various angles: listening to birdsong and contemplating bird behaviour; wandering through forests or the city; standing still in wetlands or out on the seashore. We will learn to look at the shape of bird beaks, to find familiar patterns and colours in foreign birds, to think about flight and wonder about the ancient lineage of birds. The activity of birdwatching can itself be a form of mindfulness, calming both heart and mind.

We may wonder sometimes what the natural world will be like for future generations. The human destruction of habitats through agribusiness and urbanization, the pollution of oceans with plastics and poisons, and the careless use of pesticides are all pushing some species over the edge into extinction. The human era of geology now known as the Anthropocene is in danger of becoming host to one of the greatest extinction episodes in Earth's history. Will there be any birds left for our grandchildren to see, apart from perhaps some urbanized feral pigeons, feeding on handouts and human rubbish?

We have a duty to take responsibility for the health of the natural world. When we do not acknowledge that responsibility, it is because we have not become truly mindful of the fact that we too are part of nature.

Whose
Swallow?

It is not uncommon for us to dream of flying. Free from the tug of gravity we glide down a hillside or across the landscape, feet no longer engaging with the earth; a half-lost memory of liberation lingers when we wake. Birds are the free spirits of the natural world – agile, aerial inhabitants of the rich environment we all share. Much of their attraction lies in the way they come and go in their own time, unhindered by fences, unrestrained by weight. Deep down, I suspect, we envy their ability to fly.

Birds do not belong to a particular place, though they have their own wide territories. The birds that we feed do not belong to our garden, although we may see them there regularly and talk easily of 'our goldfinches' or 'our hummingbirds'. We may even come to recognize some individuals: the friendly bird that watches as we dig the garden or becomes very interested in the compost we spread around the roses. But open the garden door and the birds on the feeder are off in a flash, disappearing into bushes or over the hedge and away. They take flight and vanish. The same rapid dispersion happens when a hawk casts its sinister shadow cruising low through the garden on the hunt for a meal.

A WORLD WITHOUT BORDERS

Many birds do not even belong to our country or continent, never mind our gardens. Their annual migration raises an interesting question. Are the swallows that nest in the eaves of homes in northern Europe, European birds, who wisely spend their winters in Africa – or are they African birds who fly north in time for the spring insect fest and the hatching of their chicks? Are the hummingbirds that buzz around the feeders in Arizona, American birds – or are they South or Central American, because that is where they migrate to in winter? The answer of course is neither – or both. Birds know no boundaries that appear on our maps, but come and go as they please, driven by behaviour evolved many thousands or millions of years before human beings invented politics or nation states. It is salutary to realize that the world is not ours alone, and it is unreasonable to treat it as private property.

It can be hard to imagine the extraordinary journeys that migrating birds make annually, crossing oceans and continents, linking distant places. The thought of tiny warblers flying thousands of kilometres is baffling: we wonder how they have the energy or the resilience for their journeys; what inner urging it is that drives them on; how they find their way. But, despite our difficulty in identifying with their experience, they help remind us that we live in a global ecosystem; nowhere is isolated, no species independent of all the rest. We are all part of one vast web of life.

A NEW PERSPECTIVE

One way to learn respect for the global migration of birds is to follow them – as William Fiennes did, recording his 5,000-kilometre journey with the snow geese in a book of that name. He begins his quest in Texas by the Gulf of Mexico, where the geese over-winter, gleaning for leftover grain and grubbing for the roots of sedges and grasses. Restlessness builds up in the geese as they respond to the urgent call of their internal clocks, eventually taking to the sky in enormous clamouring flocks, forming long skeins and 'V's as they embark on their annual journey north. Fiennes follows their ancient flyways across the United States to Canada and on to their Arctic breeding grounds on Baffin Island, reconnecting with them at staging posts where they stop to graze. It is an extraordinary journey, full of mindfulness and delight.

There are many other ways to gain some mind-hold on the borderless freedom experienced by migratory birds. Travellers between northern Europe and Africa, for example, have the opportunity to see many familiar birds from back home in an unfamiliar setting. They can seem strangely out of place to us at first, but the birds themselves are completely at home. Wagtails are as happy bobbing around the rocks of cold mountain streams in Scotland or Scandinavia as they are chasing flies on a Kenyan lawn. Swifts and swallows are as much part of the natural scene skimming the skies over an African cattle ranch as they are above the rooftops of northern European cities. An old friend of mine, the wheatear, that small blue-grey, apricot-breasted bird with a black eye mask that I have often watched bobbing ahead from rock to rock on a northern English hillside, flashing his white rump, seems equally content scanning the sky for insects from his perch on a lump of elephant dung in the African bush. Perhaps he is even the very same bird?

The
Bird Hide

With a heightened sense of anticipation you approach
the bird hide. What will you see? Whether you are
exploring an Audubon reserve in Santa Fe, or a
wetland site hidden away in London, the hope remains
the same – like unwrapping a present. We expect the
unexpected; something new, something unfamiliar,
a visitor, a migrant, a rare species – or simply a great
view of some well-known birds, near at hand and
unaware of our presence.

The approach to most bird hides is similar the world
over. A secluded path leads to the back of the hide;
a fence or hedge to each side of it conceals you from
the wildlife beyond as you make your way quietly

towards the low hut. You enter. The interior is dark, restful. To whisper feels obligatory, as it might in a church. There may be a poster on the back wall illustrating which birds are regular visitors, and a notebook and pencil for you to contribute any interesting observations. Benches around two or three sides of the hut offer somewhere to sit and contemplate as you gaze out through the low window slits, your eyes adjusting to the light and the expanse of forest or wetland before you. There may be a window shelf on which to rest your elbows as you steady and focus your binoculars.

LEARNING TO BE STILL

There is something mindful about the design and purpose of a bird hide. It encourages us to be watchful and aware. It provides the opportunity to stop and stare; to take stock of where we are in the here and now; to let go of any troublesome anxieties from past or future. It is a place, above all, to be still.

From this quiet standpoint, you check out all the birds to be seen. If you are in a wetland hide then it may be some cormorants perched in the distance, several species of duck dabbling out on the water, perhaps even an unexpected sighting of a rail lurking among the sedge so close to the hide that at first you overlooked it. A harrier drifts over the reed beds far off to your left. Nothing particularly new, you conclude, but all well worth watching.

MINDFUL BREATHING

Here could be an ideal spot in your day's activity to practise the mindfulness breathing exercise. It is simple. Sit with your feet square on the floor, your back straight (but not uncomfortably so), eyes relaxed and not searching about, but looking at whatever is in front of you. Then breathe in, slowly, naturally and a little deeper than usual. Feel the air filling your lungs; be aware of your body's need of it and its enlivening oxygen and hold it there for a moment without any strain. Now breathe out as slowly as comes easily. Repeat several times, as many as you need, your attention focused on the ingoing and outgoing breath. Quietly dismiss all other thoughts – tell them to come back later. Here you are, now, in this present moment, content to be where you are, enjoying nothing more than the life-giving breath as it flows in and out of your lungs.

This mindfulness exercise is a well-tried and ancient practice, not a new fad or fashion as many news items seem recently to suggest. It is one of the simplest forms of meditation and easily accessible to everyone, to the healthy and the sick, the old and the young, the troubled and the calm – to the religious and the non-religious.

The Buddha, over two and a half thousand years ago, taught 'Right Mindfulness' (*Samma sati*) to his followers as the seventh element of the Eightfold Path. He wanted them to wake up in this troublesome, transitory world and come to see things as they really are. To focus on one's breathing is to begin the process of enlightenment and growth in wisdom.

You may now want to turn your attention back to the birds, your appreciation of them enhanced by your renewed inner peace and focused awareness. At that moment a family explodes into the hut; noisy children race for the seats, chattering excitedly. Your peace is disturbed? No, certainly not – that is if your mindfulness moment was true. Inner peace observes the boisterous noise of the world and lets it be. How good it is, you reflect, that parents introduce their children to birdwatching, even if teaching them to be still will take a little longer.

Forests
and
Foraging Flocks

It was one of my first birding walks on my own up into the woods. I must have been seven years old at the time and without binoculars. A green woodpecker had come to intrigue me. His moss-green back and yellow rump, scarlet skull cap and strong beak seemed to come straight out of a book of exotic foreign birds. He would bore into the ground with his beak and then look up, surveying the field for intruders, then hop forward and bore again. When finally disturbed, the bird headed with undulating flight up into the trees on the flanks of the hill above. It was his laughing call that drew me up into the woods on my own. I had to climb over a wall and push my way through undergrowth to reach the deep, silent spaces between the tree trunks.

For a while nothing happened. Hundreds of ants busily carried twigs and scraps of leaf, building a large anthill by a rock not far from where I stood. Then a great tit appeared, exploring a branch close in front of me; blue tits followed, a tree creeper, a pair of chaffinches – all foraging for insects, twittering and chattering among themselves. I watched, entranced. I had found a new world, and at the same time observed my first foraging flock of small birds.

WORKING AS ONE

The foraging flock may contain up to a dozen different species, all finding safety in numbers. They have discovered that cooperation – one of the great ignored themes of nature – is better than going it alone. They move through the undergrowth and the canopy as one, from trunk to trunk and branch to branch, a feathered army on the pillage, working together. All the time they keep in touch with their calls, twittering and chirruping in pace with their busy search for insects and grubs.

TUNE INTO THE FOREST

One of the great benefits of birdwatching is not just the discovery of the birds themselves, but also of the environment around us; we see and experience it with new eyes and an enquiring wonder. When we look for birds in the forest, we are entering a new world, surrounded by some of the oldest living things on Earth. The primeval forests of the world are sadly shrinking though logging and careless agribusiness. Even so, there are still a great many forests, patches of deep woodland or wild scrub scattered about the globe. Forests are essential to the planet's health, breathing oxygen into the atmosphere and holding the soil together in times of flood; their biodiversity is rich and valuable. The mindful birdwatcher will want to explore them at every opportunity, for they are integral to the world we live in.

At first, it is not easy to see birds when they are surrounded by trees and undergrowth, shaded by an overarching canopy of branches and leaves. We might walk for half an hour and see nothing; perhaps a single jay will flash between the trunks with a screech, or a woodpecker may disappear behind a tree as soon as sighted. But this is not wasted time. The experience of being among the trees is worth savouring for its own sake. We take time to look about us, noticing the different types of trunk, the textures, patterns and colours of bark; we inhale the smell of leaf litter and wet loam, the agreeable stench of fungi. Places like this existed long before human beings evolved on the planet; forests are home to so many species of birds and other life. We let the forest wrap itself around us, mindful of its rich diversity. 'Forest bathing' is much talked about these days; the supposed healing properties of time spent in woodland is perhaps related to the chemicals emitted by the trees for their own protection from infection.

We spend time absorbing the quiet atmosphere of the forest, becoming more aware of ourselves as a single part of the scene, one life form among many, when something begins to stir. Small birds appear, exploring crevices in the trunks, hawking for insects and leaf gleaning. We may think the forest is empty of life, when suddenly we are surrounded by a mixed feeding flock working its way through the undergrowth. The variety of species in the flock will depend on where we are in the world; you never know – there may be a local rarity among them. The foraging flock is always well worth waiting for.

Cassowaries
and Company

We live in an ancient world. All living creatures, including us, are the product of a three-billion-year process of evolution. Birds, the successful descendants of one branch of the kingdom of dinosaurs, have a multi-million-year ancestry as old and as noble as that of the mammals. We humans are latecomers to the scene, having emerged from the mammal kingdom only relatively recently. Birdwatchers are a new phenomenon on Earth, something worth remembering when we set out for a walk with our binoculars.

It can be a great strain on our imagination to grasp the immense time periods of nature's history. Geologists will attempt to illustrate and illuminate the task by talking about the slow processes of mountain building and erosion; about the layers of sedimentary rocks beneath our feet, laid down over long eras as ancient seas ebbed and flowed across the land; about the slow drift of the continents, measured in centimetres per century. We struggle to comprehend what is being said, even when we have learned to repeat the figures involved.

ANCIENT ANCESTRY

The lengthy biography of bird evolution can help the ornithologist gain some purchase on the nature of deep time, and our own place in it. Nowadays, guidebooks to birds begin with the oldest families in terms of their evolutionary lineage, and move on through the book reflecting the order in which each species is thought to have evolved, right up to the newest arrivals on the scene, the passerines, or songbirds. So, in a copy of Lars Jonsson's beautifully illustrated *Birds of Europe*, the order starts with divers and grebes, petrels, shearwaters and cormorants, and ends with the buntings.

However, recent research into DNA has shuffled the recognized order. We discover that the divers are no longer the oldest species, and have been replaced by wildfowl and gamebirds. The buntings have also lost their place to the New World warblers. These New World so-called warblers are now considered to be the most recently evolved of all birds, having experienced an explosive period of speciation in recent history.

A CONTEMPLATION ON DEEP TIME

But it is a certain family of birds, the ratites (comprising ostriches, emus, rheas, cassowaries and kiwis), that really help us grasp the miracle of evolving life on our planet. Despite all the reordering of species, the ostriches and company have retained their place as one of the world's oldest bird lineages. Only to be found in the southern hemisphere, these birds are strange creatures; they are all flightless and far removed in appearance and behaviour from the songbirds that frequent our bird tables.

The ostrich is probably the best known of this ancient family. It has the unfortunate reputation of being rather stupid, burying its head in the sand when faced with a problem, but this is a folk myth, and quite untrue. To see this magnificent bird is an unforgettable sight: two and a half metres tall, with black plumage, strong legs and a haughty neck, it surveys the landscape with the confidence of a creature with no enemies. Far from being stupid, the ostrich is one of the great survivors of the savannah. It can outrun enemies with the speed of a racehorse or defend itself with a powerful kick.

The ostrich's ratite cousins all display their own unique characteristics: the kiwi in New Zealand snuffling through the leaf litter at night like a hedgehog while whistling to his mate; the emu running through the scrub of Australia's outback; the shaggy-coated rhea stalking among the thorn bushes and long grasses of South American plains. Arguably the oddest of all is the cassowary, a rare and dangerous man-sized inhabitant of the rainforests of Queensland, Australia, and the island of New Guinea. This dinosaur of a bird has razor-like claws, a bone-like crash helmet, blue face and heavy pendulous red wattles hanging from its throat.

These distant ratite cousins are all flightless, with feathers that have the appearance of coarse hair. They are descendants of a common ancestor who lived in the ancient supercontinent of Gondwana over a hundred million years ago. As that vast landmass fragmented, the movement of the tectonic plates carried the pieces slowly apart, no faster than the growth of our fingernails, to give us the continents which we know today. And on each of these pieces, the flightless ratites evolved differently. Such changes only happen through deep time, and the ratites have seen it all.

As we contemplate in awe the lineage of this ancient family, and reassess the ages of other bird species, it can be salutary to recognize our own species' very recent emergence in the ecosystem of the planet, and to appreciate and cherish our place in the miracle of evolving life.

On Keeping a
Journal

Many ornithologists keep what has become known as a 'life list', a list of every bird that they have seen both at home and in their travels. It will probably be subdivided, for example into local birds, European birds, North American birds and Asian birds, with sub-lists of wetland birds perhaps, or migratory species. Some list-makers will subdivide even further, recording birds only seen within their own gardens (hesitating about whether to include those seen from the garden in a neighbour's plot!) Some will focus on the birds of a specific family – hummingbirds, raptors, plovers or honeyeaters. The making of lists seems to be an ingrained and addictive human activity.

Apart from the private pleasure these lists may give the observer, they can also have a useful purpose. Many ornithological societies, both local and national (such as the Royal Society for the Protection of Birds in Britain, or the Audubon Society in the United States) keep a mindful eye on the distribution of birds and of the waxing and waning of their numbers. The information gathered has immense importance for our understanding of the effects of global warming and habitat loss, of pollution at sea and urbanization on land. Anyone feeling drawn to this sort of work should get connected with a birding society, to help us all become more aware of our place in the ecosystem.

RECORDINGS OF NATURE

Arguably the most famous recorder of his observations of nature in the Western world was the eighteenth-century English clergyman Gilbert White. He set the example for birders by faithfully recording the comings and goings of birds in his Hampshire parish in the south of England, noting their habits and the dates of arrival and departure of migrants. Through careful observation and correspondence with other ornithologists – his brother lived in Gibraltar – and with contacts as far away as Senegal in Africa, he was able to make a great discovery. It was popularly believed at the time that swallows did not leave Britain in the autumn but hibernated in the winter, in the nooks and crannies of cliffs and in the mud at the bottom of ponds. Crosschecking with others, White was able to conclude, correctly, that the birds in fact migrated between Europe and Africa (though he still believed that some might hibernate).

White's book *The Natural History of Selborne* became one of the most published books of natural history in the English language. His home in Hampshire has become a focus of pilgrimage for many; the study has shelves from floor to ceiling stacked with multiple editions of his one book, and a stuffed bird, named after him, sits on a mantlepiece – White's Thrush.

THE ART OF
LOOKING AND LISTENING

Keeping a personal journal has a different purpose to keeping a life list. Part of the deep pleasure in seeing a new bird is in recollecting the observation later, recalling the scene, replaying the inner video. Writing about it in a journal is an act of revision, enhancing the memory, preventing the experience from vanishing into hazy and uncertain past. It also teaches mindful awareness, making us more alert to the rich and colourful fabric of the present moment, training us in the valuable art of looking and listening. Make the note on the same day – or even within a few days – and you will be surprised at the amount of detail that comes to mind unaided. Leave it too long and the memory begins to fade: 'Was it a double wing bar I saw – or single; and what colour were the legs?'

In a personal journal, the briefest note can, years later, trigger a rich memory, details one had forgotten flooding back. Almost 20 years ago I was walking though palm savannah in Paraguay, making my way back to the estancia where I was staying. I stopped to listen to the drumming duet of a pair of giant woodpeckers silhouetted against the evening sky a kilometre away. 'It was an evening for duets,' I wrote in my journal, 'a yellow-rumped cacique began to whistle his three clear rising notes, leaping to a higher note then dropping. I imitated him several times and he became interested, moving closer through the bushes. As the sun softened into a red ball on the horizon, a pair of turkey-sized southern screamers whooped and cried together somewhere in the grassland far behind me.' If I read that passage again today, I am transported back to the track, and find myself seeing and hearing other things I had forgotten – the sounds of cicadas and frogs, the call of distant owls and the black vultures settling on the farm fences for the night.

Birdwatching
Without
Binoculars

Sometimes it can be a good thing to leave the
binoculars behind. A non-birdwatcher might not
understand how hard this can be; we birdwatchers tend
to cling to our binoculars, and automatically carry them
on any walk. They bring a bird up close, revealing
details and colours that would be missed by the naked
eye, helping immensely with identification, enhancing
our sense of wonder. A pair of good binoculars, chosen

with care, can be a birdwatcher's most prized possession. But observing a bird through binoculars is a very different experience from seeing one with the naked eye. The field of view seen though lenses is limited, isolating the creature from everything else. For a moment we are lost in our focus on a remote branch, or a patch of water out on a mudflat.

The value of 'binocular fasting' is that we experience the birds around us without magnification; we, as observers, share the scene with them, and we are all – human beings, birds, wind and sky – part of the same living moment. We become more aware of ourselves as part of the world, more mindful of the mystery of our own being.

TAKING A FAMILIAR PATH

A local, well-known walk, one that is familiar to us and where we already know the birds, offers a useful opportunity to give the binoculars a rest. We will lose nothing by it. If our binocular-free walk should take us out onto the seashore, we may see and hear a flock of piping oystercatchers fly low above the waves or a little band of scurrying sanderlings dodging the incoming tide; we may observe a flock of gulls exploring some seaweed-covered rocks, or a cormorant flying overhead. We breathe deeply and taste the fresh sea air, soaking up the scene, the repetitive lull of the waves and the wide sky.

Where I live, in Britain, a well-loved walk takes me through woodland and down a lane. In the woods a treecreeper, small as a mouse, shuffles up the moss-covered trunk of an oak, while woodpigeons make an explosive clatter as they take flight. Emerging into a lane I hear the agitated call of a blackbird and a flock of starlings swirls past overhead; I hear the rush of their wings and watch them plunge behind some trees. Perhaps there is a sparrow hawk in the vicinity; I wait and watch but it remains hidden. A robin sings from its perch in the hedge, liquid song raising my spirits, and a wagtail, bobbing, scuttles after insects on a distant farm roof. I take note of the hedgerow plants – cow parsley and tufted vetch maybe, depending on the season; if the hawthorn is in bloom, I stop to examine the tiny flowers that cover the bush in a snow-like blanket. Fresh butterflies bring me to a standstill, as they dance along the bank ahead of me.

None of the birds observed on these familiar walks need to be identified using binoculars – we already know them well and recognize them even when they are far off. Often it is their behaviour that gives them away, their 'jizz' in the language of birdwatching. Both they and we are part of the same natural world, breathing the same air, partners in one lovely web of life. We do not need binoculars to become aware of ourselves as observers, as part of the scene; we do not need binoculars to feel grateful for just being here.

OBSERVING WITH ALERTNESS

What we find, in birdwatching without binoculars, is that we become more mindful of ourselves in our role as observers; we too are part of nature. As we become more alert, we take a greater interest in our surroundings, noticing aspects of nature we have up until now blanked out. It might be birds at our feet that we have always ignored.

Feral pigeons, for instance; we scarcely give them a second thought in the modern city, despite their varied and interesting colours, from black through soft greys and browns to white, often with a delicate iridescence about the neck. But should their white rump catch our attention, we might recollect that this pigeon's ancestor was a rock dove. In Britain, many such doves were captured in Scotland a century ago and shipped in crates down to London where they were released at weekends for pigeon-shooting parties; some escaped, survivors in their struggle for existence, and found a refuge among the buildings of the city. From there, they spread – like sparrows – to other cities of the world; the high windowsills and ledges probably reminded them of home. We and they have become city dwellers, belonging together, surviving in a new urban era.

Woodpeckers
of the
World

Few birds show more character than the woodpecker, humorous subject of cartoons the world over. The bird's profile is instantly recognizable when clinging upright to a tree trunk – often with a flash of red feathers somewhere on its body, sometimes with a perky crest – hammering away at the wood using its powerful neck muscles and strong beak. The busy activity of a working woodpecker can be a wonder to watch. We have a special feeling of pride when one appears in the garden, an exotic visitor from a wilder place. Easily disturbed, it flies off with its iconic, undulating flight.

There are over 200 species of the family Picidae, the woodpeckers of the world, and they have adapted to live almost everywhere from the coniferous forests of the tundra to the tropical rainforests of Africa (although remarkably there are none in Australia); they inhabit moist temperate woodlands and dry savannah, deserts, grasslands and mountain slopes. They live for the most part by drilling into the bark and crevices of trees and dead timber, searching for grubs and insects; some specialize in ants for their diet, others in acorns, while others suck the sap of trees. There is rich variation both in colouring and size; the smallest are the minute piculets, no larger than small warblers, while the largest can be up to half a metre in length.

NATURE'S CARPENTER

The high-speed tapping of a woodpecker is often the first thing to draw our attention; move too fast, hoping to see the bird, and we may be just in time to witness it disappear round the far side of a trunk. They are shy creatures and do not like being watched when at work, although sometimes we may be granted a special and memorable view. I had the privilege of one such experience on an early morning jungle walk in Argentina near the famous Iguazú Falls. I had heard some slow tapping from a dead tree by the track and stood still to watch. A hole high up caught my attention; a scarlet-crested head appeared, then a large black bird emerged, looked about, and immediately re-entered the hole. It was the robust woodpecker. I was then entertained by the sight of the head reappearing regularly to chuck a cascade of wood chips down onto the track, rubbish that this chiselling carpenter had accumulated from its nest excavating activity.

Come the mating season and male woodpeckers (occasionally females) indulge in another high-profile activity: drumming. They select a dead branch or a hollow log, sometimes a wooden telephone pole, anything that will resonate well with sound, and proceed to drum loudly on it at high speed. This is a different activity from hacking away bark for bugs or digging out a hole for a nest. It is to advertise himself and attract a mate. One is bound to wonder why the bird does not get a headache – but apparently evolution has blessed him with a well-padded brain.

AN INVISIBLE WONDER

One of the most intriguing features shared by many woodpeckers is invisible to most birdwatchers: its tongue. When extended, it is much longer than the beak, but it spends most of the time coiled up inside the scull. It has a barbed and sticky tip, ideal for extracting ants or other insects from deep holes drilled into logs, anthills or the ground: it hauls them in with a flick.

The amazing design of the woodpecker's tongue is something that attracted theologians in the past; it was once thought to be conclusive proof of the existence of God. The English clergyman William Paley (1743–1805) was the author of a much-read book, *Natural Theology or Evidences of the Existence and Attributes of the Deity*.

It was favourite reading of Charles Darwin, before Darwin came up with his own theory of evolution by natural selection. Paley's argument rested on the idea that evidence of purposeful design in nature implied that there must have been a designer, just as surely as the complex workings of a watch pointed unerringly to the existence of a watchmaker. 'Design must have had a designer,' wrote Paley. 'That designer must have been a person. That person is God.' The woodpecker's tongue had a part to play in Paley's thinking. The tongue might have been lengthened over generations of use, Paley agreed with other natural philosophers of his day, but what of that useful barb at the end? 'These barbs . . . are decisive proofs of mechanical contrivance,' he concluded. For him they were proof of God.

Whatever view we may take of a divine creator, we cannot avoid, when contemplating a woodpecker, being struck by the miraculous and creative power of the natural world. Our awareness of the here and now becomes tinged with astonishment.

Bird
Names

Success! Got it! You have identified the bird – a new one not seen before. Your suspicions had been raised when you first glimpsed it in a bush: you had noted the size and colour, the bill shape and wing markings, the way it appeared and behaved (its 'jizz' in the language of birding) – enough to pin it down later, in the guidebook, and give it a name. The thrill of such a moment is known to every birdwatcher.

The need to name things stems from a deep urge in humanity to understand the world, which is our home, in all its rich diversity; to recognize and respect other creatures as fellow mortals, and by naming them to acknowledge their unique individuality. Even the earliest writers of the Bible recognized the human need to identify things, believing that God commanded Adam, the first man, to name all the creatures. The human urge to understand the world comes from our not wanting to sleepwalk through life, ignoring the environment that surrounds us as though it was irrelevant to daily life, but instead wishing to be mindful and engaged with the rest of nature. We may also suspect that we have a responsible role to play in the time we have on the planet.

WITH CLOSE LOOKING COMES PLEASURE

The value in being able to give a name to a bird comes with the essential focusing that is needed to identify and distinguish the bird from others like it, to notice and enjoy its individuality. In the eighteenth century for example, little buff or greenish leaf-gleaning songbirds known as willow wrens appeared in the hedges of northern Europe in spring. By watching carefully, birdwatchers began to notice some subtle differences in the birds' song, leg colour and markings above the eye. The willow wren turned out to be three separate species: the willow warbler (with flesh-coloured legs), the wood warbler (with a yellower breast) and the chiffchaff (with dark legs). Giving them names helped observers distinguish the birds in future. Learning a name becomes a way of noticing; it helps us to look searchingly, with all our critical questioning faculties engaged. And with close looking, comes pleasure.

BRINGING ORDER TO DISORDER

A tidying-up process has taken place in the identification of birds, to address the wealth of new and colourful names generated by local lore. The British lapwing, for example, is also known as the peewit, or 'green plover'; in some places it is called the 'horn pie', elsewhere the 'flop wing'. To make life more complicated, there are other portfolios of alternative names in other languages, multiplying the problem many times over.

Added to this entertaining confusion are the names bestowed by New World settlers in the past; well-known bird names from the newcomers' old country were given to roughly similar species in the new land. Often, modern-day birdwatchers have been surprised to find that the American robin is in fact a thrush; or that the Australian willie wagtail is not a wagtail at all but a fantail, which wags its tail from side to side rather than up and down. And the Australian magpie, although black and white, is not from the crow family at all but is a butcher bird with an entirely different call (sounding, it has been said, like an angel gargling).

In the eighteenth century, a Swedish natural philosopher Carl von Linne (1707–78) began the process of bringing order to the naming of birds. Linnaeus (as he is now known) developed a systematic method for classifying birds, plants and other animals. He came to be known as the father of taxonomy; a popular cartoon of the time portrayed him as Adam in the Garden of Eden.

Linnaeus' new scientific approach to the naming of creatures is a binomial system, whereby each species is given a genus name followed by a specific name. The birdwatcher in this system is *Homo sapiens*, *Homo* being the genus we share with other, now extinct, humans; *sapiens* indicating that we consider ourselves to be the wise ones of the bunch. The common blue tit has the scientific name *Parus caerulius*, thus distinguishing it from its cousin the great tit *Parus major*. With the Latin names, the ornithologist can compare observations, easily, with colleagues from abroad.

But the names are not all. The birdwatcher will do well to heed the advice given to the world-famous physicist Richard Feynman by his father: 'See that bird? You can know the name of that bird in all the languages of the world, but when you are finished, you'll know absolutely nothing whatever about the bird.' His advice was that you had to really look at the bird, to see what it was doing. By naming the bird we differentiate it from others – and that helps us to look.

The Magic of Birdsong

Of all the species of bird in our forests and woodlands, savannahs and wetlands, it was the songbirds, the passerines, which emerged from their branch of the evolutionary tree most recently. How lovely for human beings that this should be so. We have the full-throated nightingale and the thrush, the mockingbird and the lark ascending, all singing lustily in our time: our era on Earth is enhanced by their song. Many a poet has been moved to write of an individual bird – Walt Whitman, Keats and others.

One aspect of learning how to live mindfully is to learn how to listen. We touched on the ancient mindful breathing practice in The Bird Hide (see pages 16–21).

That exercise was designed to bring us into the present moment by focusing on the in-and-out breath, to make us feel comfortable in our own bodies; mindful breathing helps us to slough off the inner world of anxieties, worries about the future and concerns about the past. It deepens our awareness of being alive now.

TUNE INTO NATURE

Learning to listen can have a similar effect. The birdwatcher out in the natural world is well placed to explore this area of experience. It may entail shutting our eyes for a few minutes, or, while walking, switching attention from the windows of our eyes, to focus on what we can hear. Farmyard sounds from the distance may come to our ears, the drone of a high-flying aeroplane, someone chopping wood, the wind in the trees, the barking of a dog, the patter of approaching rain. Best of all perhaps is birdsong, both close at hand and remote: a lark carolling from on high can be deeply moving. Much of the time we shut out all these sounds.

The call and song of birds is a great undeserved gift; become acquainted with it and we open up a new approach to bird identification. Often it will be the bird call or a snippet of song that reveals the identity of the singer. There is a useful app for this that can be downloaded to a mobile phone – although personally I prefer to linger and listen long enough to build up my own inner reference system. Once you have identified a bird by its song by yourself, it is hard to forget. It becomes an alternative way of knowing.

GREETING THE SUNRISE

Rise early, very early, while it is still dark, and we can witness one of the great wonders of the natural world: the dawn chorus. After a break without eating, often huddled against the cold, birds wake and burst into song as they greet the sunrise. In town and countryside, they proclaim the day from treetop and chimney pot, in woodland and open field, particularly in the spring. The volume of sound can be quite astonishing. And as the birdwatcher knows, the early morning can be the best time for observing, when the birds are up and about busily feeding.

In Native American mythology, the dawn chorus has long been recognized as a special event. The Jicarilla Apache creation myth recounts how the most powerful of the spiritual beings, Black Hactcin, after making the animals, created the first bird by mixing soil with a drop of rain. This pleased Black Hactcin, so deciding that the bird needed companions, he grabbed it by its feet and whirled it around in a clockwise direction until it became dizzy, its head filled with strange images and dreamlike forms. When the bird recovered, the dreams had taken shape, and there they all were – eagles and sparrows, hawks and herons, hummingbirds, swifts and crows.

The birds quickly became anxious that one day Black Hactcin would leave them, so they asked for a companion to care for them, a human being. Black Hactcin agreed to the request and sent the birds and animals out foraging for all the materials needed: white clay, black jet, red stone, opal, red ochre and dark clouds for hair. He then marked an outline on the ground, an outline just like himself, and put all the gathered materials into it. He summoned the wind to enter the moulded form and the wind left whorls on the fingertips where it entered the body.

While this magic was happening, the Black Hactcin had commanded the birds and animals not to look – but the birds, in twittering excitement, could not resist the temptation and did look, causing the magic to go slightly awry (which is why some of us appear a bit odd!) Nevertheless, they all burst into exuberant song when the first man came alive, as they still do every morning with the dawn chorus.

Beaks
and Bills

Birds, not having hands to bring food to the mouth, have been cleverly provided by nature with a whole toolkit of strong beaks and slender bills to do the job – and much else besides. Every bird, even the simplest or dullest, is exotic in its own way, a miracle of design in its adaptation to the environment.

With their purposefully designed beaks, birds can chisel out deep nesting places in tree trunks, or weave delicate receptacles for their eggs with moss and spiders' webs, grass and feathers; they can preen their own beautifully designed feathers to keep them healthy, waterproof and flight efficient. They can carry food to a safe place to consume it, or turn their eggs to regulate the temperature. They can break open the shells of snails and molluscs to feast on their tasty occupants, chip away tree bark to forage for insects, drill the ground for worms, ants and bugs galore.

KNOW THE BEAK, KNOW THE BIRD

In the identification of a bird, the shape of the beak can be an important element in tracking down the species we have observed. The bird is so much more than merely a replica of the photo or painted illustration in the bird book; it has an active life, with its own special behavioural profile – a profile much influenced by the useful shape of its bill. To know the bird truly, we need to be aware of far more than its static image. By taking particular note of its beak, we become more aware of the way it lives, and deepen our mindful appreciation of nature.

When we are new to birdwatching, the significance of beak shape may come to our notice for the first time when trying to sort out and identify different birds. The warblers, for example, have small, delicate bills suitable for gleaning insects from leaves, whereas buntings, finches and sparrows have stronger beaks ideal for cracking seeds. As our knowledge of birds increases, we learn to distinguish, from among the water birds, the sawbills (such as mergansers, with a long, serrated bill perfect for gripping a slithery fish) from ducks, which have softer, broader bills designed for scooping up pond weed. Once we have grasped that much is to be learned from the shape of a bird's bill then we will be in a good position to appreciate the more exotic designs on display. We may marvel at the crossed mandibles of the crossbill, ideal for twisting open fir cones to extract their seeds; or gaze with admiration by a river at the stiletto bill of the heron, perfect for spearing frogs and fish.

THE GREAT THEORY OF EVOLUTION

The wealth of bill variation is wonderful, from large to small: the long, iconic curve of the curlew, ideal for probing the mud; the spatula-shaped bill of the spoonbill, swinging from side to side, sifting shallow water; and the multiple variations among hummingbirds, each adapted to probing particular flowers. But all this variation is not merely a source for marvel, or an aid to identification: it was the varying shape of beaks that provided a clue for one of the great discoveries of the nineteenth century, Charles Darwin's theory of evolution – the great living process that produced all complex life on Earth, including human beings, as well as all the birds of the world.

Part of Darwin's role as naturalist on his trip round the world on HMS *Beagle* from 1831 to 1836 was the collection of data and of specimens – it was acceptable in those days to shoot birds for ornithologists back home to examine. Among these specimens were finches from the remote Galapagos Islands off the coast of Ecuador in the Pacific Ocean; slightly different species of finch, with different shapes and sizes of beaks, were found living on different islands (technically they are not finches at all, but related to the New World tangers). At the time Darwin was unaware of their significance, but fortunately his servant – who did most of the shooting – labelled the collection island by island.

It was only much later that it dawned on Darwin that these birds were a perfect example of the mechanism of evolution that he had discovered: natural selection. Darwin had inherited from his grandfather Erasmus the belief that all life evolved on Earth, but no one was quite sure how it happened. Natural selection was the answer. Darwin's finches had each adapted to their own island's environment and evolved depending on the food source available. Some birds' beaks were adapted to catching insects, rather like warblers, others to seed eating like true finches; one species with an enlarged beak even adopted the role of a woodpecker.

Darwin's discovery was a mindful moment for mankind. His reflections on the way beaks evolved strengthened his insight into the origins of design in nature. And the creative processes that shaped the beaks of birds through evolution, we now realize, also shaped us, the birdwatchers.

Who Follows?

There can be no more iconic image of autumn, in some parts of the world, than the sight of a flock of seagulls following the plough. The farmer turns the soil to sow the seed and the gulls flock behind the tractor to eat the worms and bugs, a moving tableau crossing the field back and forth. Birds left behind fly forward to take their place at the front, their turn for the freshest pickings – a rolling cloud of excitement.

A similar sight is to be seen at sea, as a swirling cloud of seabirds scream with anticipation in the wake of a fishing trawler, waiting for the nets to be hauled in, for the catch to be sorted, unwanted fish discarded overboard. When we witness such scenes we experience a real sense of being part of the living ecosystem. We share the world with other creatures; the seagulls belong to the present moment as much as we do. We are privileged observers but not superior beings.

LIVES ENTWINED

Some birds have become habituated to follow humankind, a natural link developing between the two species; we share our world; our lives are entwined together. After the last Ice Age it did not take long for seed-eating sparrows to discover the benefits of the agricultural revolution; now they are to be found happily chirping wherever human beings settle, in the farmyard and by the corn store, in city and village. The European robin, an alert companion to many gardeners, is happy to perch close to a human being's feet while keeping a watchful eye for worms and bugs as the soil is turned. There is strong evidence to suggest that, originally, the robin was a follower of wild boar, which dug up the turf for roots, until we came along and they transferred their interest to us. Are we in their view simply a more useful species of pig, doing their digging for them?

Sometimes we have cultivated this affinity between wild birds and ourselves for our own benefit. The hen scratching in backyards the world over, so valued for its eggs, is the domesticated version of the Asian jungle fowl. We guard the bird carefully from foxes by securing the hen coop at night.

WORKING TOGETHER

This manipulation and control of one species by another, however, is not always a one-way street. As we have seen, robins, household sparrows and flocks of feeding seagulls are well aware of our existence, and have discovered that we have our distinctive uses. But the honeyguide, a small, unobtrusive bird to be seen in the open woodland of East Africa, has developed an interesting practice that goes well beyond simply following humans around; in this relationship it is we who are guided.

Perched, often on a traditional calling site, the honeyguide remains very still for long periods of time. The first thing the birdwatcher may notice, as it flies off abruptly, is its undulating flight and the flash of its conspicuous white outer tail feathers. There are several honeyguide species in East Africa, but the one of special interest is the greater honeyguide. The male, mostly greyish brown, has a black throat patch and whitish cheeks; its binomial scientific name, *Indicator indicator*, gives a clue to its arresting behaviour.

All of the honeyguide species feed on insects – but they also love beeswax. Their problem is how to get at the wax in a bee's nest without being attacked by a wild swarm of the angry owners. The greater honeyguide is devilishly clever and discovered the solution a long time ago. When he has found a bee's nest, deep in the forest on the trunk of a tree perhaps, or on an outcrop of rock, he flies off to his perch above a woodland path and waits for a human to pass by. He then gives a call which has become recognized by the locals; once he has gained their attention, he heads off towards the bee's nest. The human, who also has an interest in harvesting the rich honey, follows. Once the bird has guided the person to the nest, it perches quietly to watch and wait.

The human, now possibly joined by others, lights a fire and wafts the smoke towards the buzzing hive, driving the bees out. As the humans raid the nest for its honey, the honeyguide quickly drops down to glean the wax, as confidently as a robin waits for worms when the gardener turns the soil. It is probable that this crafty little bird worked together with honey bears at first but has extended his remarkable behaviour to include *Homo sapiens*. Through the honeyguide, we become aware that cooperation between species – a major theme in the successful working of evolution – is a tactic we could do well to adopt in our relationships with the rest of nature.

Enemies

Not everyone appreciates or has respect for the birds of
our world; for many people they may be no more than
a nuisance, or even an irrelevance. Others may regard
them as gun fodder for the sport of game shooting.
Of equal concern is the habit (illegal in many countries)
of some gamekeepers of snaring, poisoning or shooting
the raptors of the area – the harriers, buzzards and
golden eagles. Their loss is tragic and unnecessary.
Biodiversity and the balance of nature badly need these
beautiful creatures. We should not forget, too, that they
have their own right to exist. It is their world just as
much as it is ours.

Then there is the annual slaughter of small birds as they migrate in spring, across the Mediterranean. The practice is defended on the grounds that it is a traditional right – but without any consideration of the changing world we live in and the increasing threat to the planet's biodiversity. A mindful appreciation of the birds we watch has to include an understanding of a wider picture of the world we inhabit. A rich web of life has evolved on this planet, a whole spectrum of species from microbes to mankind. We who have power must learn to live in a sustainable way that shows respect for all other life forms, recognizing the valuable part they play in the balance of our ecosystem.

A PLANET UNDER THREAT

Many bird species now face extinction because of human negligence. There was a time when the word 'extinction' brought to mind the flightless dodo of Mauritius, the lumbering three-and-a-half-metre-high moa of New Zealand or the great auk of the Arctic – all of them hunted for their meat and wiped out. The situation is now far more serious.

Whole swaths of wildlife face oblivion because humankind is having such a transformative impact upon the surface of the planet. We are facing potentially one of the greatest extinction episodes in the history of our world. Global warming, for example, quietly shifts ocean shoals of sand eels further north, depriving massive colonies of puffins and Arctic terns of food for their chicks. The destruction of natural habitats through logging and monoculture takes away the arboreal world that is home to many colourful Asian songbirds. The pollution and poisoning of the oceans throughout the world with waste and plastic rubbish gives us heartbreaking images of albatrosses regurgitating plastic bottle tops for their starving young. The universal use of pesticides and herbicides by agribusiness protects crops, but also clears the night air of moths and the fields of the buzz and hum of insects – with untold ill-considered consequences.

THE GIFT OF INSECTS

We give little thought to insects most of the time; we might think it mildly eccentric if we witnessed someone waving a placard proclaiming 'Save the mosquito!' Unlike whales or tigers, the protection of insects does not figure high on our list of priorities. And yet it is insects who are the great pollinators of our food crops around the world, and it is they that have given us the flowers that make a paradise of our hedges and forests, meadows and mountains. A hundred million years ago the pollination of trees and plants was mostly effected by the wind. But then evolution explored a new area of cooperation and the world of flowers emerged in co-dependence with insects, with bees and flies, moths and butterflies. What a gift!

Birdwatchers are not immune to the irritation of insects. Swarms of midges in the Scottish Highlands can be a terrible distraction when trying to observe a red-throated diver out on a loch, or a raven on a crag. Ravenous mosquitoes can surprise the unprepared birdwatcher visiting northern forests and tundra in Canada and elsewhere. I have personal experience of similar horrendous clouds of biting insects in Paraguay, where the mosquitoes drill though jeans and shirt. Wrapped up and suitably netted, wearing thick rubber boots in the heat and the humidity, I must have looked a strange figure. Holding binoculars steady when watching one of the many species of tyrant flycatcher, while mosquitoes feasted on my knuckles, ears and eyebrows became an exercise in disciplined self-control.

The unregulated use of pesticides and insecticides is the greatest enemy of the insect world and presents us with a looming crisis. The world was alerted to this potential catastrophe as far back as 1962 by Rachel Carson in her famous book *Silent Spring*. Insects have a valuable role to play in our complex ecosystem – the planet cannot do without them. Apart from anything else they are part of a chain of being that provides food for a wonderful wealth of insect-eating birds whose loss would be tragic.

Variations
on a Theme

One of the great pleasures of birdwatching in foreign parts is the discovery of a familiar type of bird exhibiting a subtle local variation, either a subspecies or a separate species – recognizably the same, and yet different. It is like the enjoyment we experience on hearing the variations on a theme of music, an improvisation on a melody. So, visitors to the Guadiana River in southern Spain, for example, may chance upon a sparrow nesting amongst the basketwork mass of sticks in the base of a stork's nest. He is just like the familiar house sparrow with its small black bib, except that this bird has a chestnut crown and the bib extends right across his chest and upper belly. It is the Spanish sparrow.

Evolution, the great generator of life across the planet, is rich and creative in its response to opportunity; through natural selection, it continues to create new bird species by working from amongst the fittest of any generation, in any given environment. It seems to flourish when it can explore new ways of expressing a form, exploding and improvising into variations in size and colour, diet and song. So, for example, we do not have just a few birds in the tit family, also known as the chickadees. European birdwatchers are familiar with the tiny blue tit, and the great tit, the long-tailed tit and coal tit – and many more besides. But travel to the Himalayas and we will find wonderful variations: fire-capped, rufous-naped, spot-winged and grey-crested tits and others, all recognizably from the same family but with variations that have evolved as they spread around the globe. In North Africa, we may observe a subtler variation of the common blue tit, a sub-species with a much darker blue crown.

LOOKING FOR THE DIFFERENCE

The 'peewit' call of a northern lapwing as he flops around the sky like an old-fashioned aeroplane from World War One, curling and diving above open ploughed fields, is well known to anyone in Europe who loves birds. Seen up close, on the ground, the iridescent feathers of his back are a mysterious mix of purple and green; his narrow crest raised, he is ready to fly up with a clamorous scream if we approach his nest. In West Africa the crowned plover plays the same role out on the open plains, grass airfields and cultivated land. He is similar to the lapwing but has no crest, unlike his common cousin the black-headed plover. They both fly up in the same agitated way as their northern counterpart, noisily proclaiming their territory and protecting their young. Cross the world to the plains of South America and there we find the spur-winged lapwing, exhibiting all the same characteristics, with some variation in markings. Recognizing the type is strangely pleasing and warming!

By contemplating this burgeoning bounty of nature – observing how it cannot help but play with shape and colour, explore variation, improvise on old themes – we become more aware of the amazing process of evolution. We have emerged from it ourselves alongside the birds we watch; we are both part of a dynamic, developing ecosystem. Some see this process as driven solely by chance; others understand it to be the work of a greater intelligent power, utilizing chance in the process of creation. Whatever our belief, we cannot help but be struck by the wonderful creativity exhibited in the natural world.

THE HAND OF GEOGRAPHY

Two other examples – the spinebills of Australia, and the bluebirds of North America – can help us be mindful of the surging tide of nature and deepen our understanding of what is slowly happening around us. Spinebills are members of the large family of honeyeaters. The eastern spinebill of New South Wales, Australia, has a long, thin, downward-curved bill designed by nature to probe tube-like heath flowers for their nectar. His throat is white with a rufous spot at the centre, and his belly a wonderful apricot. The western spinebill, to be found on the far side of the country, is similar, although the spot on his throat is expanded into a large and rich chestnut patch; he has a little white eyebrow. The two types of spinebill have both evolved through the selective pressure of geography; separated by the great Red Centre and the vast and arid Nullarbor Plain, each has developed differently.

Similarly, if we should travel across North America we will observe subtle changes in the colouration of the bluebird, from deep azure in the east to purplish-blue in the west, each sporting varying amounts of chestnut on the breast; the mountain version of the bird is blue all over. These variations are a result of the breadth of the country and the isolating effects of the Wisconsin ice cap during the last Ice Age. Nature, it seems, does not miss an opportunity to explore new forms of beauty.

City
Birds

No one who lives in a city and who loves birds should
despair. It only requires a small effort to discover that
the urban environment provides many opportunities
to pause in the rush of life, to stand and stare while
watching a bird, to value the moment. Just as the city
can be rich in all it has to offer the enthusiastic walker,
by way of alternative and varied routes, so it is also
packed with discrete habitats for wild birds.

Many wild birds have found a comfortable home
in the growing cities of the world. The blackbird for
example, that great songster, hails from the forests of
central Europe. His song has evolved to be loud and
clear in woodland, so enhancing his claim to territory.

But now he has moved into the city, with its ample food supply in urban gardens and parks, and his melodious song dominates the dawn chorus, rising well above the sounds of early morning traffic. He is just as much at home with the noisy human turmoil as is an oven bird as it struts the pavement in Buenos Aires, Argentina, or a rainbow lorikeet exploring the verandas of an apartment in Sydney, Australia. Even more surprising is the peregrine falcon, the fastest of all birds, who hurtles out of the sky above sea cliffs or wild moorland to stun his prey, and is now to be found successfully nesting on cathedral spires and the ledges of downtown skyscrapers. There are plenty of feral pigeons around to keep the falcons and their chicks well fed.

HAVENS IN THE CITY

Most cities sport great waterways: rivers and canals, docks and marinas – all wonderful places to relax into the present moment, to discover what has been described as the 'radiance of the here and now'. Often it is the very presence of a river that has allowed the city to grow, providing a handy means of transport, with barges carrying materials and produce for the growing population. These waterways with their fish and eels, mud and reed banks, create an ecosystem that is very attractive to birds. Walk along the towpath of a canal or the bank of a river and we are bound to see varieties of gulls, grebes and geese, ducks and swans, cormorants, herons, moorhens and coots. They are made easier to observe because they have become quite used to the passing traffic, inured to the presence of fishermen and joggers along the riverbank, boats plying upstream and downstream, the general busy hum of urban life.

Many cities boast wonderful botanical gardens, each with its own rich flora and fauna. Wander, for example, among the cycads and proteas of Kirstenbosch in Cape Town, South Africa, and paradise flycatchers can be seen in the tree canopy; red-eyed doves strut about the flower beds, while brimstone canaries flit amongst the bushes. In the eucalypts of King's Park in Perth,

Western Australia, a tawny frogmouth rests on a branch, while a rufous whistler opens its throat to the sky with the most beautiful of songs – 'amongst the most joyously exuberant of all Australian birds', according to a local guidebook.

Everything is different again in Singapore's botanical garden, where the heat and the humidity build up during the day. Amongst the magnificent blooms of the three-acre orchid garden, we may see yellow-bellied sunbirds with black throats, myna birds, glossy starlings and bulbuls; on the lake are white-fronted water hens and little herons. Higher up the botanical garden there are towering rainforest trees where we could be lucky enough to glimpse a colourful dollar bird, the prominent white spot on each wing revealed as it flies up from its perch. It is easy in such a place to recollect that our planet hosts a rich and glorious ecosystem.

If a city has no botanical garden then it is sure to have a cemetery. Graveyards, perhaps paradoxically, are full of life – so long as they have not been too well manicured. They provide a quiet haven away from the noise and bustle of the city. Yew trees in particular offer safe places for small birds such as goldcrests and kingbirds to glean for insects. A wild cemetery may well support whole families of sparrows and songbirds, owls or woodpeckers.

A HELPING HAND

Birds are marvellously adaptable in their behaviour and they have no problem finding food and security in the presence of high concentrations of people, which is why it is so important that we cooperate with their willingness to live alongside us. Bird tables and hanging feeders, cleaned and supplied with food (particularly in cold weather), make a great contribution to the survival of local birds. We may build up quite a large company of regular dependent visitors. The appearance of a hawk, cruising lethally though our neighbourhood, although initially upsetting, is ironic proof that we are doing the right thing.

Wetlands

It is the wide, open skies of most wetlands that are part of their charm and attraction; low horizons and generous cloudscapes dominate the experience of the birdwatcher; distant birdcall is carried on the wind. They may be bog or fen, marsh or swamp. Down by the shore they are the broad mudflats revealed daily by the tide, and open river estuaries regularly flooded from the sea. The world needs its wetlands for the wealth of life they support; they are home to a rich biodiversity, where aquatic plants flourish and bird life is abundant. Wetlands lighten the human spirit, too. It is in these watery worlds, while feeling part of the landscape, that we can become more aware of our oneness with nature, mindful of our role as privileged observers in a world we need to care for.

There are some wetlands where it might be wise and even necessary to go with a guide or join a birding party: swamp forests and mangrove wetlands, for example. Personally, I enjoy birdwatching on my own and feel faintly uneasy joining a chatty party of binocular-carrying people. However, there are times when it can be essential and prove to be greatly rewarding. The Caroni mangrove swamp in Trinidad is an example. I wanted to see the phenomenal scarlet ibis and the only possible way was to join a guided group. This took us by boat one evening down mangrove-festooned waterways into a wild paradise of life and colour. Many varieties of heron stood sentinel on mud banks; egrets and clapper rails stalked in the shadows, while tyrant flycatchers flitted amongst the vegetation. Perching upright on a dead tree was a bird with an extraordinary camouflage, looking like a stick of old, dead wood: the common potoo. I would have missed it had not our guide pointed it out. He also drew our attention to a sleeping boa constrictor wound around a branch as we passed close beneath.

All this was a rich prelude to the unbelievable sight of hundreds of scarlet ibis flying in to roost in the trees for the night. The colour contrast between the scarlet birds and the bright green mangrove leaves was startling; they looked as though they had emerged from the imagination of a surreal artist. I would not have missed this wetland trip for the world and I could not have done it on my own.

A WETLAND PILGRIMAGE

Every birdwatcher should, if they are able to, treat themselves to a personal pilgrimage to see an elegantly flamboyant wild flamingo in its natural wetland habitat. A little research will easily find places where they congregate in shallow saline or alkaline waters. One of my own favourite spots is by the shores of Lake Boringo in the African Rift Valley, where they flock in enormous numbers. To witness a million of these tall and slender wading birds, pink and white on coral pink legs, sifting the soda waters of the lake through their perfectly adapted bills, is an unforgettable experience – a display of nature at her most colourfully creative.

There are many other birds to see at Lake Boringo, one of which, by contrast with the glorious flamingo, is perhaps the ugliest bird in the world: the marabou stalk. It is equal in size to the flamingo, with a massive grey bill of hard horn and a naked pink scrofulous-looking head and neck with a grotesque pendant throat pouch. A gregarious scavenger of offal, it often consorts with vultures by animal carcases. It stands by the flamingos in sinister silence, awaiting a wounded straggler or the death of a bird. Another visitor to the shores of the lake, exploring the rocks and mud by the reeds, is the unpretentious common sandpiper. Wherever we go in the world, by lake, river or seashore, the common sandpiper pops up, often on his own. It is almost as though the same bird follows us around the globe!

AT ONE WITH NATURE

My own fondness is for the wetlands that lie around the coast of the British Isles. Here, it is easy to feel at one with the natural world. The sound of a flock of piping oystercatchers lifts the spirits. You may hear them before you see the black-and-white birds flying low, rapidly, along the beach to settle on some rocks where they immediately start to explore for shellfish, probing the seaweed with their strong orange bills. In the distance a curlew calls with its beautiful liquid notes that are designed by evolution to carry on the wind. They are the sound of the wetland itself, along with the wind, the piping of ringed plovers and other small wading birds. And there again, slightly separated from the crowd, is the common sandpiper!

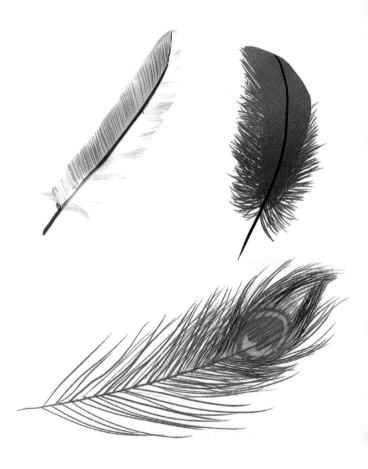

The
Feather

Find a feather; hold it in your hand, blow on it and let it drop: it floats in the air. So light! The feather, unique to birds, is a miracle of efficient design. Take a moment to appreciate the mystery of such a wonderful creation.

The quill, so useful to our forebears for writing, is hollow; it provides the main shaft of the feather, strong but almost weightless. Hundreds of barbs like smaller feathers grow out from the central vane, forming the gentle sheet of material that allows the feather to float down easily on the air, like a leaf. The barbs are flanked by many thousands of smaller barbules, each with many hooks along their sides. If the feather should be damaged in flight, the bird merely needs to draw its beak over the

ruffled area in preening and the barbs all zip up
and heal the delicate structure. Feathers make flight
possible; they can also be waterproofed with oil
from the preening bird's glands. Without the zipping
structure they become 'down', providing effective
insulation beneath the outer feathers.

The creative evolution that made the feather is truly
remarkable. Human technology could not have devised
anything better. As we contemplate this natural
phenomenon, we become mindful of the fact that we
live our lives immersed in a living mystery; we are just
one branch of the extraordinary emergence of life on
the planet.

THE FIRST FEATHERS

It is thought that feathers first evolved on small
dinosaurs, the ancestors of today's birds, being more
effective at providing warmth than scales. Delicate but
unambiguous feather structures have been found in
fossils from that era. We do not know when colour

became part of the design, but it is conceivable that fancy feathers then played a big part in courtship and sexual selection. A male driven by hormones to show off his colourful coating may have discovered that a bit of dancing and leaping about helped in the seduction of a mate. Feathers on his arms would allow him to leap higher and higher, until one day flight was discovered; arms became wings. The females would be very impressed and the DNA for the more elaborate and flight-worthy feather would be passed on. Further advantages from the discovery of flight then became central to evolution – for opening up new areas for food gathering, for providing warmth and protection from extremes of weather, and for allowing a rapid escape from predators.

IN PRAISE OF COLOUR

The spring plumage of birds, males resplendent in their courting colours, is well recognized, and anticipated, among birdwatchers. We learn to identify birds in their different states of dress both before and after their annual moult. But the bright new colours of spring are not always the result of new growth. The male redstart, for example, looks very different and much less distinguished in the summer months, and it is only when the ends of his throat and breast feathers become worn away during winter that they reveal the lovely black throat and rich rufous breast of spring. It is a lovely change brought about through wear.

Many of the more colourful feathers that have evolved in nature, from egrets to eagles, jays to orioles, pheasants to exotic birds of paradise, are so beautiful that they became the chosen adornments for a new arrival on the evolutionary scene: human beings, with their penchant for fashionable hats and headdresses. The emblematic tail of the peacock (actually covet feathers – the true, rather ordinary tail lies beneath) with its rich greens and blues, startling eye patterns and fan-like display, is an extravagant example of how far nature will go in supplying birds with an advantageous means of competition in courtship.

A wonderful variety in the patterning of colour helps to identify the owner of a feather found on the ground; variegated or vermiculated, barred or plain, all are arrestingly beautiful, each in its own way. But there is one form of feather colour that catches the eye in a particularly startling manner: iridescence. We witness this only when it is presented to us from a particular angle: subtly on the necks of some pigeons, vividly on the backs and wings of many species of glossy starling in Africa, and memorably from the throats, cheeks and crowns of many hummingbirds. Nature creates colour in feathers through colour pigments. Black pigment is especially robust and appears in the wing tips of many birds, protecting them from wear. Iridescence, however, is created by fine ribbing on the surface of the feather which breaks up the wavelengths of light, reflecting them selectively. We have a real sense that the bird is signalling to us as we watch. By observing the bird we help create what we see; without an observer the colours would be missed.

Sunset
Wonders

There is an ebb and flow of life in the twilight skies of evening. The swallows and martins make their final forays for insects in the fading light, dashing hither and thither; the screaming swifts cleave the air for the last time before nightfall. No sooner have the birds gone to rest, roosting in their nests or on wires, or sleeping on the wing if they are swifts, then the darkening sky is inhabited again, this time by the night shift: by small flying mammals, bats, hunting for moths, mosquitoes and other insects that frequent the dark.

We – birds, bats and human beings – all share the same evening air, and yet how different are their worlds from ours. As we stand and breathe the evening and then night air, we become more deeply aware of the world we inhabit, astonished perhaps that we had no part to play in our own existence on the planet. We are here in the present moment and can only feel pleasure and gratitude.

TAKING TO THE SKIES

A creative urge running though our ecosystem utilizes every opportunity offered by chance and circumstance, in a most wondrous way. Flight has been discovered by evolution several times on this planet: first were the insects, including the giant dragonflies; then came the pterodactyls in the age of dinosaurs, followed by the birds, emerging from another branch of the dinosaurs with their innovative flight feathers; last of all, mammals took to the skies in the form of bats and flying foxes. Now in our twilight sky the bats take over from the birds in hawking for insects, guided by sound rather than sight: an aerial display of silhouettes flitting against the fading light.

In the evening skies of Sydney, Australia, another change of shift takes place, a two-way traffic to and from the city. During the daytime an enormous congregation of large fruit bats hangs asleep in several trees in the botanical gardens at the heart of the city; wrapped in the thin black hairless webbing of their wings, they look thoroughly sinister. But at nightfall they stretch and chatter and head off to the outskirts of the city, a great ragged company of Halloween silhouettes, to binge on figs and other fruit. Meanwhile, heading in the opposite direction to these commuters, a massive flock of dramatically large black cockatoos make for their inner city roosting sites before dark; their flight is slow and buoyant on big, floppy wings.

AN EVENING PERFORMANCE

We should always keep an eye out for the pre-sunset behaviour of birds: there is a lot happening as they prepare for the night, finding a safe roost, catching a last snack before hours of forced fasting, sorting out a refuge from bad weather. Some behaviour may come as a surprise: on a winter walk in Europe we might come upon a large flock of female chaffinches in a thorn bush, all facing west as their fluffed-up feathers absorb the last rays of the setting sun, sharing a communal need to get warm before dark.

The flocking of starlings in the evening has become well known, as hundreds of thousands of birds – a great 'murmuration' – sweep and dance about the sunset sky in close formation. They become as one, a blob of darkness mysteriously held together as though by telepathy – a living, shape-shifting, amoeba-like being, twisting and turning at great speed in unison in the fading light. Why they do it and how they accomplish their aerodynamics remains something of a mystery at which we can only marvel. And then suddenly, as if in response to a hidden instruction, the show comes to an end and the birds fall out of the sky, funnelling down to roost noisily in a reed bed or beneath a seaside pier.

Wherever one happens to live there will be something to look out for, a local evening performance, as birds prepare for the night. If you live near a river estuary as I do, then the evening sky will become a river of gulls as they row lazily down to the sea for the night, their day of grubbing for food in the fields over. In the autumn, in particular, they are joined by gossiping skeins of Canada geese heading in the same direction, aiming for the water meadows and mudflats where they can roost in safety, away from foxes and other predators; there is safety in numbers. In winter they are accompanied by other species of migratory goose and many types of duck, so that the evening sky becomes a brief swirl of activity. I first learned to love this time of day when I was 12 years old and would cycle several kilometres after school to some open wetland by the sea; here I would watch dozens of cormorants fly into the local marshes to roost for the night, black forms arrayed in purposeful formation silhouetted against the sunset sky.

The Spiritual Realm

There are moments in life when the spiritual dimension breaks through and stirs us strangely, and a bird can be as much the cause of it as any other aspect of nature. We may hear the song of a thrush one evening, the singer high on the uppermost branch of a tree, proclaiming nothing less than joy. It catches our attention and we feel an aching sense of beauty, our spirits lifted as we are transported into a realm of the sublime. We find ourselves standing still, drawn into reverent silence by this unexpected gift.

In such moments we experience a heightened awareness of the mystery of our own existence, here and now; we feel at one with the bird, the song and the evening. To be a conscious part of the scene, to be awake to such a meaningful spiritual reality, has a quality of the miraculous. The disturbing beauty of the thrush's song stirs in us deep questions about what it means to be human in the world we perceive around us.

WHAT IS THE TRUE REALITY?

A misconception runs through much modern thinking: it is that the material, physical world is totally separate from the spiritual, that the one stands in opposition to the other. The development of science, which in itself has been a wonderful thing, informing with fresh clarity our understanding of the living world from which we ourselves have evolved, has nevertheless contributed to the idea that it is the only way to view reality. Spiritual experience has been downgraded and explained away as subjective, unimportant, and possibly even delusional.

But, stirred by the beauty of a bird singing its evening song, we can take a different view, that the physical world described by science is grounded in the spiritual; the spiritual realm is the true reality in which the evolving world flourishes and grows – thrushes and trees, human beings and sunsets. A spiritual view helps us to understand better what magic is happening to us when we are transported for a moment by birdsong. Many poets, contemplating nature, express the thought that through ordinary things one may at times be overcome by a flash of the divine, breaking through into our consciousness like the unexpected iridescent blue of a kingfisher as it flies upstream. The sixteenth-century Protestant reformer John Calvin wrote that 'nature is a shining garment in which God is revealed and concealed'.

It is not possible for us to be mindfully aware of the spiritual dimension of the world all of the time. It is a truth concealed from us in those everyday activities that absorb our lives, only to be revealed in special memorable moments – moments that we should learn to cherish.

THE CONFERENCE OF THE BIRDS

Every religion has its mystical branch, a perennial philosophy that delves deeper into the nature of being, into what it means to be me. In Islam it is the Sufis who took seriously the idea of a hidden spiritual reality lying within and behind what is familiar: they used the language of allegory to explore and explain their experience. A mysterious being, the Simorgh bird, figures prominently in the renowned twelfth-century poem of Farid ud-Din Attar, The 'Conference of the Birds'. In the poem, a pilgrimage is made by a large mixed flock of birds, led by a wise and ancient hoopoe; the Simorgh represents God and is the goal of the pilgrimage.

In the allegory, each bird represents the faults and weaknesses of human beings. The poem explores the excuses made by men and women who, while intending to seek a spiritual understanding of life, get bogged down in selfish concerns. The nightingale wants to stay with his beloved, the parrot is seduced by his own beauty, the falcon prefers to hunt from a royal wrist, the proud partridge cannot let go of his Self, 'that whirlpool where our lives are wrecked'. Eventually, after many adventures, a determined few reach the land of the fabulous Simorgh, where they come to a mysterious lake, and make a startling discovery. They look into the water and, seeing only their own reflections, realize that far from being a flock of separate companions as they had thought, that they together are the Simorgh – each an emanation of the One, the divine creator.

The modern birdwatcher may not want to identify with the divine intoxication of the Sufi, but surely there is a truth here, that we are all of us – trees, birds and human beings – part of a single living ecosystem. The biological sciences are now telling us the same thing.

Eggs and Nests

What can be more beautiful than the small cup of moss and lichen lined with feathers and plant down, the nest, for instance, of the European goldfinch? These nests are often built at eye level among the twigs of a bush; we peer in and see the tiny, delicate, pale-blue eggs finely speckled with blotches and streaks of purple. We hold our breath, aware of their fragility. The temptation to touch and possess, to collect and keep, can be strong. Not long ago it was considered a respectable gentleman's hobby to collect eggs in their thousands. Special pieces of polished furniture, with multiple drawers divided into little boxes lined with cotton wool, were designed to proudly house the collections. Nowadays, thankfully, birds are protected by law and it is illegal to collect their eggs, however tantalizingly beautiful. We look into the nest with wonder for a brief moment and then leave, content to carry the image in the mind.

Nature has been both richly profligate and also practical in egg design: the shell's remarkable balance of strength with delicacy; the perfection of shape and colour; the sky-blue hue of the egg of the thrush and the starling, the delicate scribbles on the shell of the buntings, or the mysterious green colour of the nightingale's. The smaller the egg the more wonderful seems the tiny creation.

The patterning of blotches and streaks on the shell becomes an aid to recognition by the bird, and a camouflage from predators. The eggs of birds that nest in holes, such as woodpeckers, need no camouflage and are white; the heavily marked eggs of large sea birds that nest on cliff ledges, such as the guillemot, tend to be pointed so that they do not roll off. The more we see of such products of millions of years of evolution, the more we come to appreciate and respect the living world, and to recognize its right to be, simply for its own sake. Things that have taken so long to create deserve our love and protection.

HOMEBUILDING

The awe-inspiring variety among bird's eggs is only matched by the architectural skills of the nest builders themselves. They exemplify the creative urge that runs through all evolving life, to prepare and care for the next generation, providing a popular metaphor in the English language – 'nesting', meaning settling down and homebuilding. Every spring we are witnesses to the frenzied activity of birds, gathering moss from the lawn, twigs and grass from the hedge, lichen, feathers, mud and string. When I was very young I was entertained to find a chaffinch's nest lined with my own hair; my mother, having given me a trim, had swept up the locks and chucked them out the back door. One nineteenth-century landowning lady in England was so impressed by the work ethic of the local rooks that she ordered an under-gardener to collect barrowloads of twigs and spread them in the paddock near the rookery!

Some nests impress by their size, such as the giant platform of sticks of an osprey, added to year by year and perched high, perhaps, on a pinnacle of rock by a thundering river; in Africa, the extraordinary hamerkop, a medium-sized brown wading bird with neck and cheek feathers that give its head a hammer-like shape, builds a vast domed nest of sticks the size of a small car in the forking branches of a tree. Even stranger are the nests of scrub fowl, bush turkeys and malleefowl in Australia. These ancient birds, known as megapodes, can work for most of the year scratching up an enormous compost heap of material in which the female then lays her many eggs. The rotting of the compost generates the heat for incubating the eggs, although the parents have to work constantly, checking the temperature and keeping it steady at 34 degrees Celsius, by adding or subtracting material. The megapodes of the Indonesian island of Sulawesi have an easier job, for they incubate their eggs in the warm sand of a volcano.

TINY MASTERPIECES

The phenomenal variety of eggs and nests produced by the burgeoning powers of nature is enough in itself to bring us to a halt as we mindfully contemplate the behaviour of birds. Arguably, the most awe-inspiring nests are those woven by smaller birds. The egg-carrying cup of a hummingbird, woven from spider's web and lichen, is one of nature's most beautiful products. And in Africa, and India, it is matched by the delicate, pendulous nest of the sunbird, also stitched together from moss and lichen, the bird peering out from a hole in the side.

Are Birds
Birdbrained?

The impressive skills that birds betray in the design and building of their nests is an ability that is often attributed to instinct. But labelling the activity as instinct tells us nothing about what is happening in the bird's own experience. Is the nest-building skill a mindless activity encoded in the bird's DNA, rather as a robot can be programmed to perform a complicated task? Or is the bird consciously aware of what it is doing as it collects materials, then stitches and weaves them into the appropriate shape? And does it learn from its experience? In our attempt to become more aware of ourselves and the world around us, we need to become more alert and questioning about the birds we observe. By patiently watching their behaviour, focusing on what is there before us, we are practising a useful form of mindfulness.

A common European Jay – a bird that has successfully found its way into many city parks and gardens – has been seen to behave in an intriguing way. High above the traffic of a main thoroughfare, the jay has been observed hopping along the branch of a plane tree with what appeared to be an acorn in its beak. After examining a number of cracks and holes in the bark, it found a small cavity where a branch had rotted away, and thrust the morsel of food into the hole. This caching of food is a well-known practice among many bird species and so is not in itself surprising. This jay, however, was not content to simply leave it there. It hopped back along the branch, plucked a leaf, returned to the hole and covered its small food supply. Was it hiding the food from others – aware, perhaps from experience, that thieving happens in the bird world? The behaviour had all the hallmarks of conscious thought.

ALERT TO THE WORLD

For much too long humans have thought of themselves as the only beings with conscious awareness on the planet. There is now ample evidence that birds behave with intelligence and are able to learn from experience. For example, in the days when foil-topped and cardboard-lidded milk bottles were left on door steps in Britain, tits very quickly discovered that they could puncture the foil and tear away the card. The habit spread so fast around the country that it can only have been through the birds copying and learning. In other words, the birds were alert to the opportunities in the world around them, a sure sign of intelligence. Some raptors in Australia have learned to control fire – they have been observed spreading wildfires with burning sticks to flush out prey. And crows, which have relatively large brains, reveal themselves to be immensely entertaining and sociable when kept as pets. New Caledonian crows from the South Pacific are the high-flyers; they have been found not only to use tools such as twigs to extract wood-boring beetle larvae from hard-to-reach places, but they even craft the tools, snapping them to the right length to make them better suited to the task.

Popular expressions in the English language reflect a rather negative view of the intelligence of birds; we talk dismissively about someone being 'birdbrained' if in our judgement they lack the ability to think logically, and we are critical of any form of education that involves 'parrot-learning', memorizing without thought. Such prejudices, however, take no account of the way in which birds communicate. A parrot, greeting the householder at daybreak with 'Morning boss!', is not a mindless automaton, but a fellow mortal, awake and alert, responding with anticipation to the appearance of the person who provides the food. In the wild, birds communicate all the time, calling others to a food source, keeping in touch, warning of predators. The patient birdwatcher will begin to recognize the alarm call that warns of an approaching cat, and the different call when a raptor appears. Researchers in Australia have discovered some very sophisticated communication skills among a species of suitably named babblers; these sociable birds have a complex system of calls which they are able to mix up and string together in order to communicate different meanings.

A GREATER UNDERSTANDING

We share the world with birds and owe it to them to try to understand the way they experience their daily lives, how conscious they are as they hunt for food and partners, build their nests and communicate. As we try to empathize with them we suffer a major handicap – the only consciousness we know about is our own. Even the consciousness of other people, of family and friends, is a bit of a mystery. But the more we become aware of the behaviour of birds the less likely we are to fall back into the prejudices of earlier times, which assumed that birds have no sense of themselves, that they are soulless, mindless creatures, without feeling, behaving as pre-programmed automata.

A Rapture
of Raptors

We both need the air, we humans and the birds of prey, the raptors. The air: we take it for granted, give it no thought, and it is virtually invisible; we see it stir the trees as a wind gets up, we feel it on our hand as we breathe out, we notice when it is polluted with industrial fumes; but for most of the time we are unaware of its presence, even though it surrounds us totally, day and night.

A basic mindfulness meditation is to focus on the air, on the life-giving breath as we draw it into our lungs and then expel it again. The practice of paying attention to the gentle rhythm of breathing, while relaxing the mind and letting go of anxieties, brings us into the present moment and peace.

HIGHER AND HIGHER

Observing the flight of a bird is another activity we tend to take for granted, rather like breathing, without giving it a second thought – that is, until we notice something beautiful. And there can be few things more arresting than the soaring of a raptor on a rising thermal of warm air. A buzzard, sometimes with companions, often flies out from a wooded valley near my garden, and begins to circle effortlessly in the sky. It is usually in spring or early summer that I notice. A couple of crows bother him, but only as irritants. With quarrelsome calling (a sound I now recognize, as it draws me outside to look to the sky), the crows dive-bomb the raptor, never quite making contact, but giving it no rest, twisting and turning as they harry their quarry like little barking dogs. The buzzard makes no more than a slight adjustment to its flight, a gentle shuffle of its tail, and continues to circle on broad wings, lifted higher and higher by the rising air, apparently oblivious to the mobbing. Within minutes the bird is carried so high that it becomes little more than a speck in the sky; the crows drop away, satisfied, and the buzzard, having gained enough height, makes a beeline for the horizon and is gone.

This rising on a thermal is a feature of flight we can come to recognize the world over: from eagles in Spain fingering the air with their spread pinions, sweeping in effortless circles as they ascend, letting the air carry them higher and higher; to hundreds of vultures swirling like a slow tornado above the pampas in South America. In their movement it is as though we 'see' the air, appreciate its presence, as it lifts the birds – and our spirits – to great heights.

IN AWE OF 'OTHERNESS'

The word 'rapture', meaning to have one's spirits captivated and raised up joyfully, is related (through its Latin root rapere, 'to seize'), to the word 'raptor'. The raptors are robbers that seize their prey: they are powerful, usually large, birds that live mostly by hunting rodents and other small mammals: this is the way they are; they are meat eaters and live by killing. A number of different predatory bird species are included in the category of raptor: eagles, buzzards, harriers, kites and vultures (from both the New and Old Worlds); falcons, caracaras, ospreys and owls; even the strange long-legged secretary bird of Africa joins the list. The physical features that bring them together in a group are their strong talons designed for gripping prey, their powerful curved beak, ideal for tearing flesh, and their acute eyesight.

Humans have always been fascinated by raptors, holding them in respect; perhaps we recognize something in their alert, self-seeking focus that reminds us of ourselves. And there is an 'otherness' about them that intrigues us. We are impressed by the stationary hover of a kestrel, a 'standing hawk', as it holds its place in the wind while surveying the ground below for mice; we are staggered by the speeding stoop of a peregrine falcon as it slices through the air to stun a pigeon.

Humans have trained these birds for hunting from the wrist for millennia, kings and sultans displaying them proudly as prized possessions.

Our encounters with raptors are always memorable, sometimes even rapturous. My first sighting of a golden eagle caught me unawares; I knew of a breeding pair in the north of Britain and went in search. While surveying the mountains and sky it took me some time to discover that the eagle had already seen me; he was perched quite close on a drystone wall, eyeing me with interest. For a moment I was an image in his world.

Pirates, Cheats
and Bullies

There is an undulating balance in the world between beauty and ugliness, pain and pleasure, cruelty and cooperation. A mindful approach to our understanding of nature will come to recognize this and accept the light with the shadow. The Buddha, when teaching the practice of mindfulness to his followers as part of the Eightfold Path to enlightenment, was encouraging them to face honestly the way things are in life; all human beings suffer pain at one time or another. Suffering cannot be avoided.

Today, recognizing that we live in an evolving world, we begin to understand that the same truth about suffering also applies to nature. All creatures suffer old age, disease and death; indeed, without death there would be no evolution to redesign and develop living creatures generation by generation. Both we and birds owe our personal existence to the deaths of millions of ancestors. Cruelty, as Darwin himself observed, is also often part of the process.

So, we become aware that not everything is beautiful in the world of birds. It is easy to be romantic about the faithful monogamy of penguins or swans; to be touched by film of an albatross greeting his mate with elaborate billing and cooing; to be moved by the devotion of hard-working parents feeding their demanding young in the nest. That is one true aspect of bird life, full of cooperation and care; we might even say love. But there is another aspect of which we have to be mindfully aware: nature is fundamentally amoral, with all creatures bent on personal survival. There is a dark side to nature often cruel and distressing that we are bound to recognize. This is the world we live in and share with all other living creatures.

NATURE RED IN TOOTH AND CLAW

The laws of nature, for example, allow for a percentage of piracy. Watch an Arctic skua pursue an Arctic tern when the latter is returning to its nest with a bill full of sand eels for its young. The dramatic aerobatics will be fast and furious, each bird a swift and agile flier – part of nature's daily dance of competition and survival. Morality does not apply here; one species of bird has simply evolved to steal, dependent on others to do the work of food gathering. Visit the Caribbean and we can witness a similar scene: magnificent frigate birds, with their forked tails and long wings resembling human beings on hang-gliders, are the highwaymen of the skies. They rob other sea birds of fish and offal; their neighbours are simply a convenient source of food.

And then there are the cheats, such as members of the cuckoo family, who force others to care for and feed their chicks by laying their eggs in other bird's nests. If all birds behaved like this it would not work – but a few can get away with it. The cuckoo has become admirably adept at deception; they lay eggs that look very like those of their chosen host, in colour and speckles. The female will fly low along a hedge or over a reed bed to find a suitable nest, then one day, when she is ready to lay, she will perch on a nearby branch and – at the very last minute – swoop into the nest, lay the egg, and be away in seconds. She has cheating honed to a fine, calculating art. Weeks later, the host parents can be seen feeding a ravenous chick many times their own size, all their natural instincts to care for their young hijacked by a greedy usurper.

The bullies can be found everywhere; adult gulls squabbling for food with younger gulls, driving them away with raucous screams and threatening beaks; crows pushing out smaller birds from bird feeders. Even among the smaller birds themselves, such as sparrows and goldfinches, we find aggressive behaviour, feathers fluffed as they explode with 'me-first' fury. And we don't have to dig very deep to find even worse behaviour. The male European robin, who becomes an attentive friend to many gardeners as they turn the soil, is a mean stickler for his territory and will drive off other males. They have even been known to kill the offspring of competitors, in order to give first place to their own DNA. 'Nature red in tooth and claw' is a true summary of much bird behaviour – that of bullies, cheats and pirates.

A MATTER OF BALANCE

With such evidence it has become fashionable to think of evolution as driven by selfish competition at all levels, the struggle for existence always ensuring the survival of the fittest. But this one-sided view ignores the balancing role of cooperation. For millions of years, the principle of working together has been as strong and important as that of any selfish struggle.

Waiting for
Spring

One of the most moving of natural phenomena in
the avian world is the regular spring migration in the
northern hemisphere, when immense flocks of birds
wing their way north to their breeding grounds. Waves
of birds roll up through the Americas; they flood across
Asia, through Vietnam and Korea; they flow from
Africa to Europe. Knowledge of this vast pageant
stirs the human spirit year by year, inducing a sense of
humility that we are part of a greater picture, observers
of a magical process of renewal.

We cannot isolate the changing behaviour of birds
in the spring from everything else that happens in that
season. The sun rises higher in the sky, warming the

ground. We breathe the fresh milder air, see leaves beginning to unfold and feel the rising sap of life. Spring is in fact more than simply the regeneration of nature, it is a symbol of rebirth and personal renewal.

SPRING ARRIVALS

The nineteenth-century American poet, philosopher and naturalist H. D. Thoreau, living in the woods by Walden Pond seeking, as he puts it, 'the tonic of wildness', listens out for the signs of spring with eager anticipation: the cracking of the ice on the pond, the sound of geese migrating north, and the singing from the fields of the bluebird, song sparrow and redwing. Thoreau's response to the birds of spring is matched by that of the wilderness sage John Muir, the Scotsman who toiled so hard to save America's wild places, founding father of its national parks. The bluebird is for him, too, the long-awaited spring arrival, heralding with its 'rich crispy warbling' a fresh year of growth and vitality.

Each of us, depending where we live, has different expectations of what birds to listen and look for. In Europe, it may be the sound of the skylark ascending above his nesting site, his winter song (a short fruity warble) transformed into a continuous flood of fluting melody from high in the sky. The lovely trickling notes of a willow warbler can bring us to a temporary standstill, enthralled. We will listen for the convivial twitter of swallows as they explore beams and roof spaces for their nests. And we will hear the cuckoo, announcing his presence with his two-tone call from some distant tree. We may forget for the moment that his long journey from Africa began in what for us was still the cold and dark of midwinter. He, with all the other migratory visitors, anticipated spring, as we do, weeks before it burst in bank and hedgerow.

The reason that so many birds fly north in the northern hemisphere in the spring is quite simple: the temperate climate of midlatitudes fuels a prodigious explosion of insects with which the birds can feed themselves and their young. But there is a worrying trend noted by many observers. A generation ago anyone driving at night in spring or summer had to contend with clouds of insects, moths and flies, splattering on the windscreen and headlights. Regular cleaning by hand was required – windscreen wipers simply smeared the mess in unseemly juicy arcs. Nowadays the car headlights no longer pick up drifts of little creatures on the night air, and the windscreens remain clean. This lack of insect life, due to the uncontrolled spraying of insecticides and pesticides, is already taking its toll on birdlife. The numbers are worryingly down.

REGENERATION AND RENEWAL

The purpose of living a mindful life is to be more aware of ourselves as human beings, conscious of our responsible place in the natural world. The regeneration of life in spring, the return of migrant birds, the renewal of plumage and the building of nests is part of a rhythm of yearly creation. We can feel it and identify with it. The religious themes of Easter (named after Eostre, an ancient goddess of the spring and the dawn) and resurrection tap into the same desire to be renewed, to start again, to move from death to life; to be awake and mindful and not asleep.

The phoenix, an ancient mythical bird, became an early Christian symbol of resurrection and renewal. I imagine an imperial, crested creature, extravagantly feathered in reds and purples, with a raptor's beak and strong talons. The phoenix was believed to live for many hundreds of years, after which he would fly to the city of the sun in Egypt, build a nest and immolate himself in a funeral pyre. Out of the ashes the phoenix would rise again to new life, like the spring, like Christ. We live in difficult times for birds – and it is mostly our fault. But the renewal of the world is in our hands. We have to believe it.

The **Gift** of **Gratitude**

I had only ever seen the bird's picture in a book, never in real life: a golden oriole. Then one day when walking through a grove of dark umbrella pines in southern Europe, I heard a lovely liquid call, 'or-io-le', and a glorious yellow bird, black tips to its golden wings, landed briefly on a low branch in front of me. I was rooted in the moment, and felt a rush of pleasure and gladness – and gratitude.

While trying to live a more mindful life it can be a great boon to discover the gift of gratitude. Gratitude can never be forced; there may be times when we know that we ought to be grateful, and may even express the thought in appropriate words, but inside we do not have the feeling. Our gratitude becomes no more than an act, a bit fake, while inside we are losing out and may find ourselves hoping that the acting will one day be replaced by something more worthy – a real, fulfilling sense of being grateful.

The natural world with all its rich beauty is a great giver and promoter of gratitude – so long as we are mindfully open to the opportunities it offers. The gift of gratitude is unbidden and wells up from within us with a feeling of joy and perhaps laughter. The unexpected appearance of a bird can have this effect. The golden oriole, that day, gave the gift. When this spiritual blessing comes to us we do well to welcome and foster it, recognizing that we have been given something good, and resolving to look for it in our lives more often. We can be grateful for feeling grateful.

GRATITUDE FOR UNEXPECTED VISITORS

Seeing a new bird for the first time can be an exciting experience, a thrill and delight for any birdwatcher. The bird may be rare; an unusual species of warbler perhaps, or an endangered macaw; it may be a common bird that somehow has never come our way before. Sometimes it is just the return of old friends that is joyful. When walking in the first days of winter near my home, with a dusting of frost on the hedgerow and a bite to the air, I might be greeted by the rough chatter of a flock of fieldfares and redwings, the first migrants of the season from further north; they have arrived in the night on a cold northerly wind. I watch them out in a field or perching in the top of a leafless hawthorn bush and my spirits rise – they are back! Feelings of gratitude blossom! This deep pleasure we can all feel at the unexpected appearance of a bird, or of a flock, whether rare or not, is often accompanied by the tingling awareness that we have been given an undeserved gift.

A MOMENT OF WONDER

Some new sightings come out of the blue – the oriole, the fieldfares and redwings – while others are deliberately sought for. I myself made a pilgrimage to New Zealand with the express hope of finding an albatross, having for many years longed to witness that ocean-sailing wonder. I found a local tourist company that offered pelagic birding trips and was taken out to sea in a small fishing boat. We speeded away from shore and quickly found ourselves out on the swell of the ocean, the coastline sinking beyond the horizon. The fisherman in charge stopped the engine and poured some buckets of fish entrails out into the sea; shark innards are particularly smelly and alluring to sea birds it seems.

Almost immediately Dominican gulls began to gather, screaming and circling the boat. Black and white Cape pigeons, a type of petrel, settled on the water around the bait, chattering to each other in quarrelsome tones. Other petrels, the white chinned and northern giant, joined them, followed by several species of shearwater. Then came the first albatross – a torpedo body with long slender wings spanning over three metres: it slid effortlessly like a glider on the air above the swell, circled and finally landed. I wondered how it managed to fold its remarkable wings; they seemed to have two elbows and close up in three dimensions. Moments later a smaller species of albatross, a black-browed mollymawk, pure-white headed with beautiful black eye makeup, joined us, dwarfing the gulls and the shearwaters. It was a moment of gifted wonder given to me from the natural world; I felt a surge of satisfaction and gladness – and, once more, gratitude.

What
Can We Do?

What can we do? We live in a period of extinctions in the natural world unprecedented in human history: the biodiversity of our world is being shredded. Bird life is suffering as much as are mammals, insects, plants and fish – and we are to blame. We are overrunning the planet, laying waste to its riches, spraying the land with pesticides and herbicides, reducing wild forests to torn landscapes or deadly monoculture, and polluting the oceans with noise and plastic. We are even altering the climate. It is easy to feel despair.

But does it matter, some ask, pointing out that species have been dying out since life began. It is estimated that 99 per cent of all Earth's living creatures have already become extinct. The extinction of a species, as conditions change on the planet, is as natural as the death of an individual, according to this view. True – but there is a counterargument. A laissez-faire attitude, one that shrugs the shoulders and dismisses what is happening globally as inevitable, ignores one thing: all previous extinction events, whether through climate change, volcanic activity or asteroid impact, happened unknowingly. Choice was not involved. We, however, know what we are doing. It takes millions of years for evolution to create something as beautiful and well adapted to its environment as a little ringed plover or an Arctic tern. Are we to allow ignorance and short-term planning to destroy such glorious creatures? Because when they are gone, they are gone forever.

A CALL TO ACTION

There is still time (but only just) for humanity to be mindful of the situation and wake up to the challenge. More and more birds appear on red lists, produced by ornithological societies around the world, alerting us to their near extinction. What can we do? One seemingly impossible task is to change the opinions of those in power, both in politics and in big business. We need to get our voice heard, through lobbying, letter writing, petition signing and voting, arguing for a switch in economics from focusing on profits to making the well-being of the natural environment the urgent priority. People with money can research how their wealth is used and opt for ethical investments, taking charge of the small amount of power they wield.

Farmers and landowners have a great responsibility, one which many are beginning to acknowledge and willingly accept. There are farmers who have adjusted the times of seed sowing and harvest to allow for ground-nesting birds to breed. Others have given up the spraying of broad field borders with insecticides and pesticides; delayed the trimming of hedges to leave berries for migrant birds; allowed wild copses, the habitat for many songbirds such as the nightingale in Europe, to remain untouched. Local authorities and those responsible for highway maintenance can be persuaded to act in similar ways, allowing common land and roadsides to flourish. In our own gardens a little wildness is to be encouraged, allowing nettles and long grass, weeds and buddleias to grow untouched, havens for insects and birds.

Education is the key to protecting the rich biodiversity of nature. We all need to be more aware of the health of the planet so we can respond appropriately in our own local patch. Just as we opt to feed our garden birds in winter, it is the indigenous people of Brazil who are best placed to protect the rare macaw, and of Borneo to become game wardens to prevent the criminal capture of songbirds for sale to collectors.

ALLOW NATURE TO TAKE OVER

One of the most exciting developments recently has been the rewilding movement, which recognizes the value of untouched areas of moorland and forest, heath and wetland. There is an urge in humanity to manage nature, to control and bring some order to it, as though it were some giant botanical garden. Much of this is well intentioned, but the more radical view of the rewilding movement is to allow nature to find its own way forward, by drawing back from trying to control and conserve natural habitats as we find them. The reintroduction of lost species of birds and of the many mammals hunted into local extinction is encouraged – but then nature is allowed to take over, to find its own unpredictable way into the future. The planet still contains great tracts of land and national parks where this exciting rewilding vision can be encouraged and sustained.

Meanwhile, we practise our own mindfulness and discover that it is not possible to be mindful of our surroundings and the birds around us without developing compassion for the ecosystem of our world. We are part of its web, aware of and responsible for the way it goes.

DEDICATION

In memory of Eric Meek

ACKNOWLEDGEMENTS

Birdwatching has been a part of my life since my parents
took me for walks across the fells, along the coast and
through the woods of Cumbria: I am eternally grateful to them
and for this upbringing. I also owe a debt of gratitude to
an old friend who died recently, Eric Meek, who was the
long serving head of the RSPB in Orkney, a man with a
deep love of the natural world, always ready to share his
encyclopaedic knowledge of birds. I would also like to thank
Kuki Gallmann who allowed me to roam for weeks, with a
guide, around her great property in northern Kenya; and
Diane and Antonio Espinoza who welcomed me often
to their ranch in Paraguay – itself a bird Eldorado.